COARSE Fishing

Written by David Holzer
Illustrations by David Miller and Mike Atkinson
Photographs courtesy of www.anglersnet.co.uk

KUDOS

Published by Kudos, an imprint of Top That! Publishing plc.
Copyright © 2004 Top That! Publishing plc,
Tide Mill Way, Woodbridge, Suffolk, IP12 IAP.
www.kudosbooks.com

CONTENTS

CONTENTS

Introduction

Today, when waters are being carefully managed, tackle is improving all the time and records are constantly being broken, there's never been a better time to take up angling.

Anglers fall into three categories: pleasure anglers who fish purely for enjoyment; match anglers who enjoy the added buzz of competition; and specimen anglers who specialise in catching big fish and gathering and comparing information.

Whichever kind of angler you are, or hope to be, there's no question that the sport demands great skill and patience. However, it's also tremendously rewarding.

Apart from the sheer pleasure of fishing, most anglers usually enjoy being close to nature and are committed to ethical angling.

This guide to coarse fishing is intended to be a handy source of reference for anglers of all types and at every level. It may also spur you on to try different techniques and broaden the range of fish you go after.

Interpreting Water and the Environment

It used to be the case that rivers were generally fished in winter and stillwaters in the warmer, summer months. Today, although modern fishing techniques have changed things somewhat, this is still broadly true, for the simple reason that you tend to get better sport fishing in winter rivers.

Also, some fish can only really be fished in particular types of weather, for example you would only fish for tench in summer. However, like most things in coarse fishing, though, this is a rule of thumb and not an absolute truth.

Successful coarse fishing starts with understanding what it means to fish in running and stillwater habitats. Even then, water conditions vary a great deal. Learning to read them is fundamental to finding different species of fish.

Weather conditions also play a part as fishing in icy weather is very different from doing so in the height of summer. Flooding, high winds and fishing in darkness also demand their own individual skills.

You also need to know where to find the fish you're after – or at least, where they should be. You can only do this by learning to read water conditions and the surrounding environment.

This introduction to the subject makes no claims to be a substitute for really going out and studying water. What it will do, however, is give you a good idea of the conditions in which you should be able to find the species of fish you're after.

7

INTERPRETING WATER AND THE ENVIRONMENT

Fishing in Running Water

When you're fishing in flowing water, the key thing to remember is that you're out there to catch fish – no matter how much you enjoy the scenery.

This may sound obvious but fish are not attracted to a beautiful landscape in the same way that you might be. In other words finding a nice spot from which to fish is not the same as finding a spot which will maximise your chances of successful fishing.

In winter, particularly, featureless and less interesting stretches of river are often the best places to fish.

INVESTIGATING SUMMER RIVERS FOR WINTER FISHING

Some anglers will only fish rivers in winter when they are at their best for species such as chub, dace, roach and pike. Although this is when they'll do their fishing, serious anglers will often investigate river features in summer when lower water levels make species easier to spot and record.

It's also simpler to spot different species of fish because they're nearer the surface of the water. Once you've spotted the species you're going to be fishing, recording their feeding places will be a good start for winter fishing.

If you really are a serious fisherman it makes sense to record your summer findings in a book that you can refer to during the winter.

Areas of smooth flow with overhanging trees, in particular, are a guaranteed spot for many species in winter.

REMEMBER

It's also a good idea, if the part of the river you're interested in is shallow, to wade it. This is the quickest and easiest way to establish what it's like on the bottom.

If the water's too deep, you can plumb all the areas where you can't see the bottom.

Where to Find Fish

Look for smooth, gravelly shallows, lily beds, deep runs under stretches of bank with overhanging foliage, rush and weed beds, underwater snags, slacks, lock cuttings, weirs, islands and bends. Investigate where tributaries meet the river.

You should expect to find one or more species of fish in any of these areas. For instance, dace, roach and grayling will colonise fast gravel and marginal rushes are typical ambush points for pike.

It's worth looking closely at depressions as that's where chub, barbel and big roach like to gather. You'll spot a depression very easily as it's likely to be a smooth area of water in the middle of the usual ripples.

It's also important to remember that you can draw fish to a specific area. River species are often nomadic but will come back to the same spot as long as the area is fed regularly in the right quantities.

Bream, for example, are nomadic and as they swim in shoals, inevitably eat all the food in a particular area. They follow well-defined feeding patterns, called 'patrol routes'.

In some rivers, anglers are able to predict when a shoal of bream will arrive in a particular area.

Vegetation

A wavy motion on the water surface usually indicates underwater weed and rush beds. Underwater rush beds split the water flow, creating two types of swim. The roots hold back the central water, forming slacker water downstream, which is a reliable place to fish for chub, barbel and pike.

Fishing featureless stretches of river in winter

A seemingly featureless stretch of river is not necessarily a bad thing. You simply need to pay more attention to the features that are there. Undercuts in the river bank become more significant, in particular.

Equally, stretches of a river that are deeper than average, sluggish and straight, can be home to some of the biggest fish. The features that are present can attract high groupings of fish.

Sunken snags on the River Severn, for instance, are a magnet for barbel. Trickles from a rivulet or land drain often attract roach while tangles of fallen branches can be a good place to find perch.

Although they're often disregarded by anglers, the shallows can be a rewarding place to fish.

A two rod set-up on the River Trent.

The Water Surface

In winter, reading the water surface will give you useful clues to the riverbed and vegetation. A disturbed surface reflects changes in underwater conditions.

In particular, it pays to look for a diverted flow because this often means that the riverbed shelves, creating a natural food trap for fish.

Creases – divisions between fast and slow water – can be caused by anything from a section of protruding bank to a marginal weed bed. Fish like variations in flow, so these are usually excellent areas to fish, particularly in winter.

Smooth areas of surface water among ripples mean hollows or depressions. In shallow water these are excellent for chub, roach and barbel.

14

The term 'constantly boiling water' refers to an area where you're unlikely to find fish. It is where the water is constantly disturbed by features such as large pieces of irregular debris on the bottom of the river.

Fish don't like being in an area like this because of the constantly changing currents.

Most anglers will tell you that an absolute must with winter river angling is to look for an area where the surface is oily and smooth and the water flows at an even pace. If you spot an area like this, it's highly likely that you have found an excellent spot for fish of many species.

A misty early morning shot taken by Julian Grattidge, which shows a four rod ledgering set-up for carp.

THE WATER SURFACE

Stillwater Fishing

It's safe to say that stillwaters present more of a challenge to anglers than running water. Although there are plenty of places to find and catch fish they're not obvious.

Pits and lakes are typically most prolific in summer which is why so many serious anglers prefer to fish them at this time. Fish may leave deep water and look for food in the shallows and at medium depths.

Angling in winter is still worthwhile even though fish are not so active, apart from pike, which become very active in clear, cold water.

GRAVEL PITS

When you're fishing a gravel pit, it's important to locate any bars, gullies, gravel plateaux, drop-offs and weed beds. Be aware that water conditions in gravel pits will vary enormously.

Clear, shallow water encourages heavy weed growth – ideal for tench, perch, roach and pike. A weed-free bottom with plenty of disturbed sediment could mean bream and carp.

In clear pits, look for areas of tree cover, islands, rush-lined bays, visible gravel bars – which attract all species of fish – and dark water gullies.

You can often locate a bar by looking for a prominent point on the surrounding land and following its line into the water.

The deepest water in many gravel pits is around margins where barges have created channels to haul gravel away. These gullies can hold a lot of natural food and you may find large shoals of roach, perch, tench and small bream or 'skimmers'.

Bird activity is another good indicator of what you're likely to find in a particular pit. Swans only feed on bottom weed that they can reach. Coots also feed on bottom weed but don't dive as deeply so their presence is a good indication of a gravel plateau. Grebes dive where there are hordes of fry, which could mean pike or perch.

In some instances – if you're considering fishing a pit with no obvious pointers, for instance – it may well be worth mapping it using a boat and echo sounder or plumbing methods.

Lakes

Lakes usually have mud or silt bottoms which can be very weedy. Bullrushes, reeds and water lilies are common and a promising sight for the angler. They provide abundant food and shelter and make excellent ambush points for predators such as pike.

RESERVOIRS

As lake bottoms tend to be relatively even and there are fixed rich feeding sites, fish in lakes are usually less nomadic than those in gravel pits.

Many lakes also have deep marginal areas overhung with bottom debris such as fallen timber. These areas can provide a haven for pike or perch as they attract hordes of fry.

There are two types of reservoir. One is created by damming a natural valley, the other by using earthworks.

Water supply reservoirs are excellent for coarse fishing. Once again, you need to establish underwater contours by looking at surrounding features.

Flooded valleys give the most interesting results. You can find original streams by looking for coloured water. These will be deeper and provide a natural current against which fish like to swim.

DAY-TICKET LAKES

Smaller lakes tend to have artificially high stock densities and it's possible to get good results from most swims, using an aggressive feeding policy.

WIND CONDITIONS

Anglers often head for sheltered areas when the wind is high but it's actually far better to fish off banks facing into the wind. Coloured water close in, caused by wave action, disturbs a lot of natural food. Strong wind will influence the behaviour of carp, rudd, bream, roach and tench, in particular. They love to feed in the shallows in rough conditions.

Coarse Fishing in British Waters

British waters are home to a remarkable array of very different species of coarse fish. Each is found in a specific habitat and particular water conditions. There are tricks and techniques for landing every one.

Some anglers become fascinated with one particular type of fish – carp fishermen are the obvious example. These anglers devote their entire angling lives to perfecting techniques for catching this species and constantly adding to their knowledge of the subject.

When it comes to fish such as pike, some anglers will return to the same stretch of water again and again, determined to catch a particular fish.

Others prefer to go after different fish at particular times of year in running and stillwaters, using a variety of techniques and tackle.

Whichever kind of angler you are, or intend to be, it's certain that coarse fishing will give you a lifetime of pleasure.

20

Streamlined pink fins ▶

Barbules either side of the mouth and snout ▶

Underslung mouth and thick, rubbery lips ▶

Small eyes, high on the head ▶

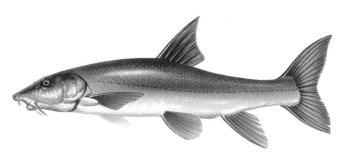

Barbel

Originally only found in fast, gravelly rivers, their popularity means barbel are now found all over England and Wales.

Barbel are members of the carp family and are mainly river fish. As they fight to the finish, they're a truly exciting match for the coarse angler.

With their sleek shape and pink fins, barbel are probably the most distinctive fish in British rivers. For many anglers, it is their appearance that makes them such an attractive fish to go after.

Perhaps the only fish that you could confuse with a barbel is a gudgeon. The most obvious difference is that the gudgeon's colour is generally duller and they only have barbules at the corners of their mouths.

MAP

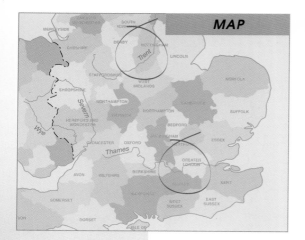

WHERE TO FISH

Although barbel were originally only found in fast, gravelly rivers they also do well in slower, quieter rivers. These slower waters are actually good places to look for individual, large barbel.

It's also the case that more and more rivers are being stocked with barbel because they've become so popular. Today, wherever you are in England and Wales you should be able to find good places to fish for them. It is, however, best to avoid commercial stillwaters that offer barbel fishing, because they're not suited to this kind of habitat.

Typical places to look for barbel include streamer weed beds, under overhanging trees, deep depressions and fast areas of water such as the tails of weir pools. If you're after big barbel, look for snags.

WEIGHT

Typical weights are 1–3.6 kg (2–8 lb). Over 4.5 kg (10 lb) is a specimen.

FEEDING HABITS

In the winter, barbel feed less but can become extremely active feeding on prey animals washed into rivers by floodwater.

WHEN TO FISH

One of the most reliable times to fish for barbel is in a warm winter flood as they're actively looking for food. This is when they will respond well to large, smelly baits like luncheon meat or lobworm.

BARBEL

Jamie Alexander displays a fine 10 lb 12 oz river caught barbel.

BEST BAIT

The ideal baits for barbel are particle baits used in quantity. These could include hempseed, maggots, tares, worms, casters, sweet corn, processed meats and sausage meat.

REMEMBER

Barbel will often fight until they're exhausted and if you return them to the river in this condition they may well die. Hold them headfirst into the flow until they recover. Or stake them out in the stream using a tube made of soft material.

Bronze bream: ▶
deep-bodied

Silver bream: rear anal ▶
and pectoral fins

Underslung mouth with ▶
telescopic top lip for
bottom feeding

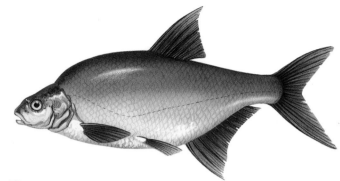

Bream

It may not be the hardest fighting fish, but with its gleaming bronze flanks and humped back, a specimen bream certainly creates an impressive sight.

Bream are one of the most challenging and difficult coarse fish to catch, especially in gravel pits.

Bream are one of the largest members of the carp family found in Britain. Although they're difficult to catch they live in shoals, so catching one could easily lead to you landing more.

There are actually two types of bream: bronze and silver. You'll be most likely to go after bronze bream, as the silver variety is comparatively rare.

Young bronze bream, often called 'skimmers' because their bodies are thin and flat, are also silver which means that they can sometimes be mistaken for silver bream. As they grow, their colour changes to be greyish brown. Some, particularly in gravel pits, can become almost black.

The best way to identify the differences between the two species of fish is that bronze bream have 51–60 scales along the lateral line and silver have 44–48.

Julian Grattidge holding a specimen bream from Capesthorne Top Pool.

Bream can turn almost completely black in a gravel pit environment.

REMEMBER

Some anglers have learned to predict the feeding lines of bream so that they can tell where a bream will be at a certain time of the day. Bream also roll on the surface before feeding which makes them easier to spot.

MAP

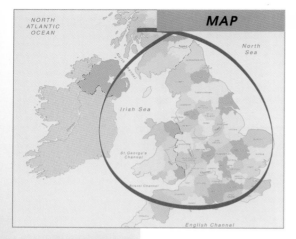

WHERE TO FISH

Bream are found all across the UK, so there are plenty of places in which to find them.

If you're looking in stillwaters, you'll find bream near gravel bars, on islands, in thick weeds and lily beds and in rush-lined bays and inlets.

In rivers, bream are found in deeper water out of the main current. Wide turning bays, overhanging cover and moored boats are favourite spots in canals.

With bream, the things to look for are muddied water and large areas of bubbles. This is because bream vacuum up their food, disturbing the bottom. If you're after big bream, the best place to look is a gravel pit.

WHEN TO FISH

Good times to fish are early or late in the day, at night and when it's humid or overcast.

You can catch bream at any time but they don't particularly like very cold weather.

BEST BAITS

Bream are notoriously fickle feeders but casters, squatts, worms, red maggots, red and fluorescent pinkies, sweet corn and bread are popular choices for anglers.

WEIGHT

With bream, there are wide fluctuations in weight. 4.5 kg (10 lb) is a specimen.

FEEDING HABITS

Adult fish will feed on the bottom, near reeds, weeds and lily pads and along underwater features.

28

BREAM

◀ Four barbules, small and large, at corners of the mouth

◀ Vacuum-like mouth

◀ Long, concave dorsal fin with 20–26 rays

Common Carp

The most popular sporting fish in Britain, many specimen anglers will only fish for carp.

Carp were once bred for food and cultivated by religious orders as one of the foods allowed during days of abstinence.

Anyone with the slightest acquaintance with carp and the anglers who fish for them will know they're a fish that can easily inspire obsession. If you decide to go after carp exclusively, there's plenty of specialised equipment to purchase and a high level of dedication to aspire to. The carp's popularity is deserved as its reputation for cunning and tremendous strength is absolutely justified.

Close-up of a perfect 28 lb 12 oz common carp, caught by Shaun Docksey.

Today, carp produced by selective breeding significantly outnumber the traditional wild variety. Wild carp are muscular with large, powerful tails.

Common carp are fully scaled; mirror carp are partially scaled; leather carp are nearly free of scales apart from a few on their shoulders and back. Crucian carp have no barbules.

WHERE TO FISH

Carp do well just about everywhere. Serious carp fishermen head for stillwaters, especially gravel pits, which hold the largest fish. In gravel pits, head for gravel bars and the margins of any offshore islands.

When it comes to other water conditions, you'll find carp in thick weed beds, under lilies, in thick cover and alongside steep or undercut river banks. Beds of silt containing bloodworm are excellent places to look for carp.

Crucian carp are most likely to be found in undisturbed water, such as farm ponds. They prefer to feed close to marginal cover and bankside rush beds.

MAP

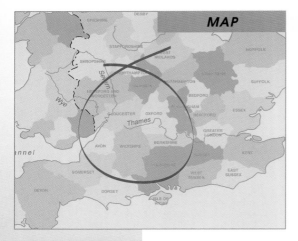

WHEN TO FISH

Carp are most active in summer months. A good tip, particularly when you're fishing water for the first time, is to fish into the prevailing wind. Carp are well known for following the wind in waters such as gravel pits.

As far as crucian carp are concerned, the best time to fish is at night, particularly the first two hours of darkness and the hour before, and the hour after, sunrise.

A favourite method of fishing for crucian carp is with an inert waggler carrying a night-light. It needs to be shotted so that the slightest lift or settling is immediately obvious.

FEEDING HABITS

Adult carp are best suited to bottom feeding and will eat anything, including snails, crayfish, bloodworms, mussels and shrimps. They also feed in mid-water and, for floating food, on the surface.

Although they're not predators, large carp will also eat other fish.

BEST BAIT

For common, mirror and leather carp use boilies, luncheon meat, sweet corn, maggots, casters, hemp and tares.

Maggots, casters, bread and sweet corn are good for crucian carp.

WEIGHT

With common, mirror and leather carp 4.5 kg (10 lb) upwards is a good fish. 9 kg (20 lb) is a specimen. Specialists aim for 13.6 kg (30 lb) or 18 kg (40 lb).

Above 450 g (5 lb) is a specimen crucian carp.

32

- Long, muscular body with small rounded tail – like a giant tadpole
- Large, flat head
- Huge mouth filled with tiny, sharp teeth
- Two feelers at corners of top jaw
- Four smaller feelers on lower jaw
- Creamy white belly, mottled flanks

Catfish

Catfish – also known as the Wels catfish – have, perhaps, the most powerful sense of smell of all coarse fish in British waters.

Most British catfish are descended from a species deliberately introduced into Britain in the late nineteenth century. In the 1960s, people began introducing catfish into British waters illegally. Today, there are only a few recognised catfish waters in the country.

Having said this, as demand for the fish increases, the number of catfish is growing rapidly.

They get their name from their whiskers, which are really feelers full of taste buds. The name is applied to any fish, including saltwater, which has feelers.

WHERE TO FISH

The best place to fish is in a weedy and overgrown lake where there is plenty of prey for the catfish.

Apart from that, fish in the margins of any water in dull conditions or at night, particularly in the south of England.

WHEN TO FISH

Fish on warm, humid and overcast summer nights in the margins, using smelly bait.

FEEDING HABITS

Catfish are scavenging predators who mainly feed at night. They have been known to eat just about anything, including dead fish, small mammals, frogs and possibly even baby water birds. It's rumoured that they'll even feed on small dogs.

Catfish have incredibly sensitive hearing and vibration detection. A catfish's swim bladder is linked to its ears which gives excellent sound vibration.

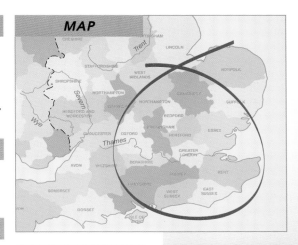

MAP

WEIGHT

9 kg (20 lb) is a specimen and 13.6 kg (30 lb) exceptional.

BEST BAITS

Livebait, chopped fish, squid, fishmeal boilies, spicy sausages, chunks of liver and heavily flavoured luncheon meats are all effective.

REMEMBER

If you're fishing for catfish, a good way to attract them – particularly abroad – is by slapping the surface of the water with a flat paddle. This is because they're extraordinarily sensitive to movement in the water.

Wide body ▶

Black-edged scales ▶

Large, blunt head ▶

Big mouth with large, white lips ▶

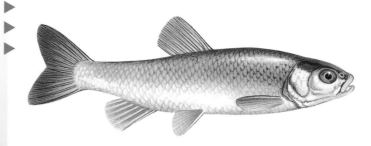

Chub

Chub have a huge appetite, are very wily and one of the best fighting fish around.

Basically a river fish, chub also do well in some canals. There are huge specimens to be found in some gravel pits, but they're extremely hard to catch.

The best time to fish for chub in rivers is between June and March. On stillwaters, you can fish for them all year round.

REMEMBER

Chub are at their fighting best in winter. They lie just off the main part of the current. An excellent place to look for chub is in places where debris builds up around overhanging branches.

MAP

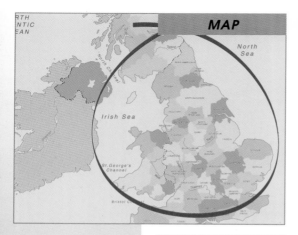

WHERE TO FISH

Chub are found in still and running waters all over England, Wales and Scotland, especially in overgrown, neglected streams. They particularly like streams where there is plenty of bank-side cover from overhanging trees and weed channels.

WHEN TO FISH

An ideal time to fish is in running water on clear, windless summer days.

FEEDING HABITS

Chub are scavengers and will eat pretty much anything at any time of year. They eat natural baits like big slugs and lobworms in winter. They'll also eat crayfish, small fish such as loach, bullheads and minnows, as well as insects that fall from the trees.

WEIGHT

2.2–3 kg (5–7 lb) is a good weight.

BEST BAIT

Try slugs – collected the morning you go fishing – lobworms, crayfish, maggots, casters, cheese paste, luncheon meat, hempseed and sweet corn.

Anglers' Net regular Gary Catchpole displays a fine chub.

38

CHUB

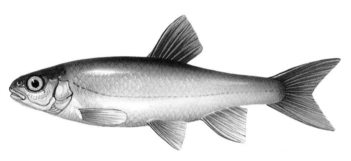

- Delicate head
- Concave anal fin
- Pale fins – from light orange to light brown

Dace

Dace feed on floating insects so they're very quick and you need fast reflexes to catch them.

Enormous shoals of dace can gather in clear, fast-flowing shallow water. Their slim bodies enable them to swim for several hours at a time in main currents.

MAP

WHERE TO FISH

It's pretty rare to find dace in stillwaters unless they're close to flooded rivers.

In rivers, large dace like deeper, steadier flows. They're particularly fond of areas of streamer weed on faster rivers.

WHEN TO FISH

Dace feed hungrily in colder weather. It's best, therefore, to try fishing for them on crisp winter days.

FEEDING HABITS

Dace feed just as well on the surface as the bottom. They take food in mid-water as well as floating insects off the surface. Dace eat water shrimp, slaters, mayfly larvae, small snails and algae.

REMEMBER

If you like a challenge, you might want to try fly-fishing for dace. They're extremely difficult to catch this way as they'll take and reject a fly very quickly. However, the sense of achievement if you manage to catch a dace using this method is well worth the effort.

WEIGHT

Any fish over 340 g (12 oz) is a specimen, but even these are rare.

BEST BAITS

When you're fishing for dace, try slugs collected on the morning you go fishing, lobworms, crayfish, maggots, casters, cheese paste, luncheon meat, hempseed, sweet corn, bread and small carp boilies.

DACE

Long, snake-like, muscular body ▶

Pointed head ▶

Dark back and creamy yellow side and belly ▶

Long, narrow dorsal fin travelling round the tail to the anal fin ▶

Eel

To many anglers, eels are a nuisance, to others, though, they're a challenge.

Famously, adult eels migrate to the Sargasso Sea – part of the Atlantic Ocean near Bermuda – to spawn. This journey can take up to three years, some of which may even be overland.

Although there are over twenty species of eel in the world there is only one, the European eel, in the United Kingdom.

Eels appear to be able to adapt as their mouth shapes vary. Some have pointed and others broad, flat mouths.

WHERE TO FISH

Look for eels under bridges, dense weed, in holes, under tree roots and snags. Specimen anglers will tend to go for stillwaters where the largest eels are found. In rivers, eels tend to be smaller.

WHEN TO FISH

Eels love darkness, whether at night or in secluded areas. They spend most of the day resting. The best time to go fishing is as night falls.

For a change, you might want to go fishing for eel on a river by sending a constant stream of maggots down from a swimfeeder.

FEEDING HABITS

Eels are scavengers and will eat fish, freshwater shrimp and snails. They feed at night and use their strong sense of smell and excellent eyesight to hunt. In gravel pits and rivers, eels will feed on the bottom.

MAP

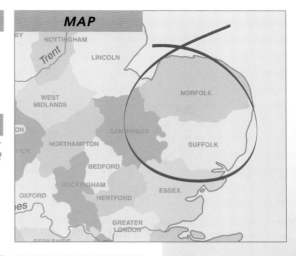

WEIGHT

1 kg (2 lb) upwards is worthwhile; 1.3 kg (3 lb) is a specimen.

BEST BAIT

Carp boilies, maggots, any animal and pungent baits are all attractive to eels.

EEL

Huge dorsal fin ▶

Silver-blue, streamlined body with violet stripes ▶

Unique, irregular, dark spots on the flanks ▶

Delicate, small and pointed head ▶

Small teeth for gripping food ▶

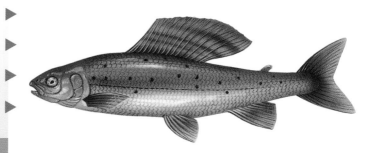

REMEMBER

Grayling of all sizes will shoot to the surface to feed on aquatic nymphs. They often respond to trotted hookbait where the float is held back so the bait swings up in the water.

They're also attracted by a regular supply of floating maggots and casters. Trotting a float is a good way to attract them when combined with this method of baiting.

Grayling

This is one of the most beautiful coarse fish – it's impossible to mistake grayling for any other fish.

Considered to be a game fish by some and a coarse fish by others, grayling are members of the salmon family. They will often thrive in smaller salmon rivers with clean, fast-flowing waters.

Interestingly enough, grayling have a smell of wild thyme about them which explains their Latin name of *thymallus thymallus*. They make very good eating.

Unfortunately, grayling are very sensitive to pollution and this means they tend to be found only in small pockets.

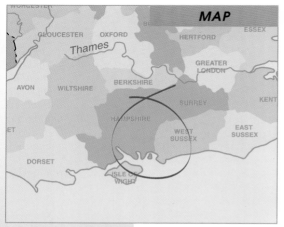

MAP

WHERE TO FISH

The grayling's large dorsal fin is there to enable it to swim in fast flows, particularly in chalk streams, and this is where you're most likely to find grayling in shoals. Bigger fish tend to hang on creases. Specimens will be found in steadier, deeper water.

WHEN TO FISH

The best time is when conditions are very cold. Clear, icy, winter days are ideal.

FEEDING HABITS

Grayling feed on the bottom but also higher in the water when nymphs and mayflies are hatching. Once grayling colonise an area they'll stay with it so it makes sense for you to check where they're feeding.

BEST BAITS

Maggots and casters. For bigger fish, use worms.

WEIGHT

Over 450 g (1 lb) is worthwhile.
1 kg (2 lb) is a specimen.

A fine grayling caught by Glen Smith at the Anglers' Net fish-in at Timsbury.

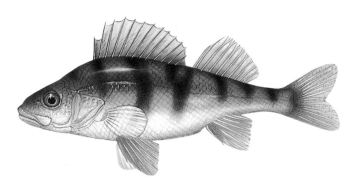

- Boldly striped flanks for camouflage

- Spiked dorsal fin – meant to intimidate predators

- Crimson anal fin

- Big mouth

- Large eyes

Perch

Small perch are often the first fish caught by the novice angler, as they're usually incautious.

Although perch are mainly found in shoals, larger specimens may drift off in pairs or even become loners.

There is only one species of perch found in Britain, although there are a number of different species worldwide, which can be found in both fresh and saltwater.

Disease destroyed the perch population during the 1970s. They are now enjoying a comeback and population sizes are growing.

© David Miller 2004

REMEMBER

Perch spend a lot of time motionless at the extreme edge of a rush bed, using their camouflage to hide and wait for small fish. For the best results, manoeuvre your bait close to the rush bed.

In winter, you could also try fishing for large perch in a deep hole on a stillwater using a ledgered lobworm. You can try the same thing in a deep undercut in a river using a lobworm on a paternoster.

48

WHERE TO FISH

Since they have large eyes, which are adapted for feeding in murkier conditions, perch don't like strong light. This is why they're most likely to be found in deep water, under overhanging cover, margins, ledges and under bridges.

In gravel pits, perch are often found on plateaux where, at dawn, they go after the fry that have spent the night there.

A good place to try in summer is near lily pads.

WHEN TO FISH

A good time to fish for perch is at dawn in summer in shallow, gravelly water.

FEEDING HABITS

Young perch hunt for small fish in schools. Perch are cannibals and are particularly fond of eating their own fry and small members of their own species.

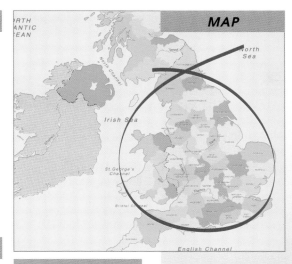

MAP

WEIGHT

1 kg (2 lb) is good as perch don't usually weigh more than 450 g (1 lb).

BEST BAIT

Maggots, pinkies, casters, worms, spinners, gudgeon, minnows and even baby perch get good results.

49

- Streamlined bodies ▶
- Deep olive back ▶
- Marbled combination of grey, green and yellow on flanks ▶
- Dorsal fin set well back ▶
- Very large tail for acceleration ▶
- Long, flat head ▶
- Inward-pointing rows of razor-sharp teeth ▶

Pike

Pike are the largest predatory fish found naturally in freshwater in Britain and attack with extraordinary speed.

Pike are distinguished by their unmistakable head and ferocious-looking mouth.

There are row upon row of tiny, needle-like teeth in the upper jaw. In the lower jaw, there are larger teeth on either side of more rows of smaller teeth. Pike also have teeth on the roof of their mouth and their tongue.

This fearsome combination is what helps pike take prey up to 25 per cent of their own body weight.

Apart from having great speed, enormous strength, ferocious teeth and extremely flexible jaws, pike use their highly developed eyesight, sense of smell and tracking system to find their prey. As they often pick off injured, sick or dead fish, pike play a vital part in balancing stocks in mixed fisheries.

WEIGHT

9 kg (20 lb) is a good specimen and 13.6 kg (30 lb) an excellent catch.

BEST BAITS

Pike respond well to herrings, sprats, smelt, mackerel, sardines and dead coarse fish.

50

PIKE

WHERE TO FISH

One of the great things for keen pike fishermen is the fact that the fish can be found in just about any river, lake, pond or pit in Britain.

As pike are predators who hunt by sight, they will be found anywhere they can hunt undetected. You'll find pike among tree roots, in rush beds and in the shadows of trees.

Anywhere in the river or stillwater bed where there is a decent depression is a good spot for pike.

They prefer to use their great speed to catch their prey through short bursts of speed rather than a long, drawn-out chase.

WHEN TO FISH

Try to catch pike on a clear, winter day after the frost has thawed.

FEEDING HABITS

Pike normally eat fish between a tenth to a fifth of their own body weight. Their flexible jaws mean that they can eat larger fish, small mammals, frogs and water-birds.

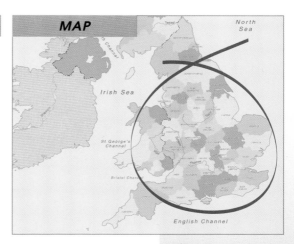

MAP

REMEMBER

The standard way to catch pike is with float tackle or ledgered bait often fitted with electronic bite indicators. A more exciting method is to goad pike into attack with spinner bait, plugs or spoons.

It's also interesting to note that pike caught using deadbaits are typically much larger than those caught using any other method. The reason, it's believed, is that all fish will become lazier as they get bigger and a pike needs to expend far less energy on deadbait than any other kind.

When you're fishing for pike, a key thing to remember is always to strike swiftly, before the fish has a chance to swallow the bait. Unless you're an extremely skilled angler, it's very difficult to unhook deep-hooked pike.

PIKE

Greenish backs ▶

Silver flanks ▶

White belly ▶

Lower fins vary in colour from yellow to bright orange ▶

Dorsal and tail fins are usually reddish brown ▶

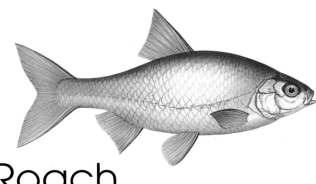

Roach

The roach is the most popular and widely distributed of all British coarse fish.

Roach are particularly abundant because they can tolerate moderate water pollution levels.

One of the good things about roach is that they can grow to specimen size in any type of water, which means you've always got a chance of catching a decent-sized fish.

It's important to be able to recognise roach, particularly the bigger fish, because they often create hybrids with rudd and bream.

The way to identify a true roach is to look at the anal fin. Roach have nine to thirteen branched rays.

55

MAP

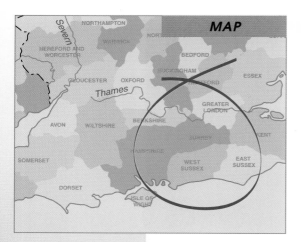

WHERE TO FISH

Go for clear, fast rivers, gravel pits, canals, reservoirs and farm ponds.

If you want large fish, look for gravel bars in gravel pits. When it comes to rivers, roach like shaded, marginal areas including rafted areas created by floating debris caught by overhanging trees.

WHEN TO FISH

For big roach, try fishing from dusk onwards in shallow, coloured waters or floods.

In summer, roach will often roll on the surface in gravel pits while in winter they gather in deep water.

WEIGHT

1 kg (2 lb) and over is a specimen.

FEEDING HABITS

Roach feed mainly on the bottom but also in mid-water and they'll sometimes come up for insects that have fallen on surface water. They eat algae, snails and bloodworms. Larger fish can become cannibals and feed on roach fry.

BEST BAIT

Bread in all forms, meat paste, maggots, casters, large carp boilies and worms.

ROACH

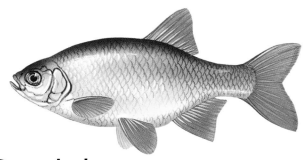

- Gold with crimson fins
- Bright yellow eyes with red spot
- Prominently protruding bottom lip
- Sharp angle from pelvic fins to tail

Rudd

Anglers, particularly those just starting out, like to fish for rudd as they take bait so eagerly.

Rudd are one of the most colourful fish in British freshwaters, with distinctive red fins.

It's a good thing that rudd are so recognisable because they tend to hybridise freely with roach. Roach are less colourful but the main difference is the mouth. Rudd have protruding lower lips, roach have upper lips that protrude and the hybrid often has equal lips.

In the case of a record fish, where it is important to establish whether the catch is definitely a rudd or a roach, the fish unfortunately has to be killed. This is the only way to examine the fish's throat teeth. Rudd have two rows, roach have only one. Hybrid fish only have a partial second row.

MAP

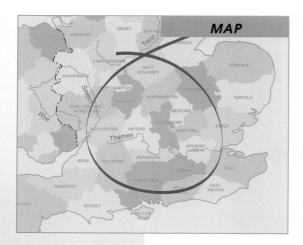

WHERE TO FISH

Head for neglected estate lakes, ponds and – in the eastern counties – gravel pits and weedy areas of canals and rivers.

It's generally the case that you'll only find large numbers in water which is rich in nutrients.

WHEN TO FISH

When the light starts to fade rudd will come out from the heavily weeded areas where they feed in daytime.

FEEDING HABITS

Rudd are mainly surface feeders and, in warm weather, lie in shoals under the surface, feeding on insects. They also take crustaceans and snails from the bottom and some vegetable matter.

Large specimens will sometimes take fish fry.

WEIGHT

1.3 kg (3 lb) is generally accepted as a specimen.

REMEMBER

Rudd will come readily to the right bait but they take fright extremely easily and need to be fished cautiously.

BEST BAITS

Sweet corn, maggots, casters, hemp and bread all get good results.

RUDD

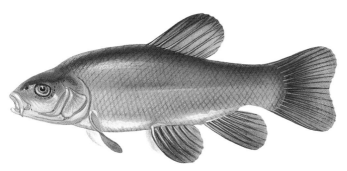

◀ Covered in tiny scales coated with heavy mucous

◀ Colour varies from almost black to bronze

◀ Lighter belly

◀ Round, paddle-shaped fins

◀ Thick tail

◀ Small eyes with red irises

◀ Larger upper lip, thin bottom

◀ Barbule at each mouth corner

Tench

Tench are a very popular fish among summer anglers but their appearance is less predictable in winter.

For many years, tench were believed to have magical powers and their slime thought to have healing properties. In the Middle Ages, for instance, it was thought that tench slime would cure headaches, toothaches and other illnesses. It was also believed that pike wouldn't eat tench, but this isn't true.

Tench are members of the carp family and their colour can vary from almost black to pale yellow. However, they normally have a deep, olive green back and flanks with a paler belly.

MAP

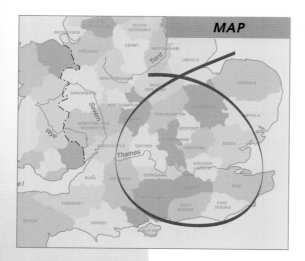

WHERE TO FISH

Good places to fish for tench include lakes, reservoirs, canals, slack bays or sluggish backwaters on major rivers.

A clear sign that tench are around is when you see large clouds of small bubbles coming up from a soft mud and silt bottom.

WHEN TO FISH

When dawn is breaking in summer, head for a bed of lilies or the margins. Tench love hot weather so you can often catch your best fish in these conditions.

In gravel pits, a good time to fish is often between 7am and midday.

WEIGHT

4–4.5 kg (9–10 lb) is not uncommon.

BEST BAIT

You can catch tench using boilies, red maggots, worms, casters, sweet corn, breadbaits and luncheon meat.

FEEDING HABITS

Tench are bottom feeders and eat anything they find – bloodworms, insect larvae, worms, snails, mussels and some small fish.

They mainly feed at dawn and dusk but sometimes feed all night.

In winter, tench barely feed, preferring to lie in the mud doing nothing for long periods of time.

TENCH

A fine 5 lb 14 oz estate lake tench, caught by Chris Knapper.

REMEMBER

Tench are territorial fish and will often stay in an area for weeks before moving on. There's no point returning to a tench swim that once paid dividends. It makes more sense to look for where the tench currently are and fish there.

Streamlined ▶

Rough, slimeless scales ▶

Double dorsal fin ▶

Large mouth with two long, front-mounted fangs ▶

Large eyes ▶

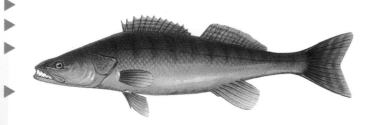

Zander

Zander are exceptionally efficient hunters, sometimes gathering in packs to feed on small fish.

A member of the pike–perch family, the zander was introduced into Britain from eastern Europe in the late nineteenth century. The species really began to flourish and become of interest to serious anglers when a number of fish were released into British waters in 1963.

Today, zander are increasingly widespread, particularly in the east of England.

Like perch, zander have large eyes to enable them to feed in murky conditions.

62

ZANDER

WHERE TO FISH

Coloured waters, near drop-offs or holes and even salty stretches of tidal river are good places to fish for zander.

WHEN TO FISH

In autumn, flood waters at dusk or night when zander have recovered from spawning.

FEEDING HABITS

Zander primarily hunt small fish like roach in packs of similar-sized fish but will also eat worms and leeches.

They prefer to hunt in lower light, as the size of their eyes would suggest.

If they get bigger, zander will hunt alone, so if you're after specimen fish it's not a good sign if you keep catching small zander.

BEST BAITS

Zander like live or dead coarse fish – particularly sections of eel.

MAP

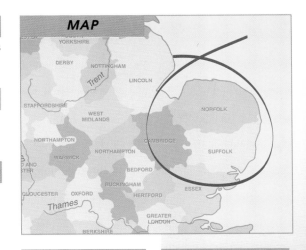

WEIGHT

1–3.6 kg (2–8 lb). Over 4.5 kg (10 lb) is a specimen.

REMEMBER

If you want to fish for zander, they're still really only found in Norfolk, Suffolk, Bedfordshire, Surrey, Lincolnshire and Gloucestershire.

63

ZANDER

Coarse Fishing in Europe

Many species of coarse fish found across Britain can also be fished for in other parts of Europe. France, Germany, Holland and Belgium, in particular, are home to roach, tench, bream, barbel and zander.

BARBEL   Barbel found in Spain and Portugal, where they can grow all year round because of the hot climate, have been landed at weights of up to 13.6 kg (30 lb).

SPAIN & PORTUGAL

PORTUGAL

SPAIN

SWITZERL

Loire

FRANCE AND THE NETHERLANDS

CARP

Most UK anglers travelling abroad are after carp, and the lakes and rivers of France are some of the favourite places to go. Lake Cassien is probably the best known destination in France for carp fishermen but Salagou and St. Quoix are also worth a visit.

Plenty of French rivers are home to carp. The River Seine, for example, has produced some large specimens.

Another favoured destination for carp fishermen is the Netherlands, particularly the canal drainage systems.

WORLD MAP

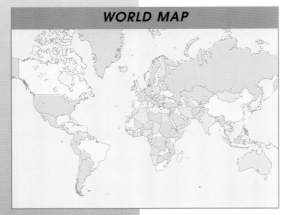

In fact, good carp are found all over the world. Intrepid carp fishermen travel as far as Australia, the Far East, Africa, the Canary Islands, Canada and America.

Carp weighing up to 31.7 kg (70 lb) have been found in Europe. In America, a species called buffalo carp can grow to over 41 kg (90 lb).

If you'd like to know more about where to find carp worldwide, how to get to the popular destinations and where to stay, contact the Carp Society for more advice.

CATFISH

Catfish over 45 kg (100 lb) have been found in France, in both rivers and lakes. Serious catfish anglers fishing in France head for: the 100 miles stretching from Lyon to Chalon on the River Saône; the River Loire between Decize and Gien; and Lake Cassien.

The River Danube is fished for catfish along its entire length. Germany and Spain are also popular destinations. Plenty of enormous catfish have been pulled out of the River Ebro in Spain.

Huge catfish are found in the Vransko Lake in Croatia.

Serious catfish anglers, however, head for Eastern Europe. The rivers Desna and Volga in Russia have often produced monster catfish of over 181.4 kg (400 lb).

As most anglers will be well aware, this part of the world can be somewhat volatile because of the political situation. It's important to be extremely careful and take advice from people who know the area when you're planning a visit.

FRANCE AND GERMANY

RUSSIA

67

SWEDEN

CENTRAL AND SOUTHERN EUROPE

PERCH

Perch over 4 kg (9 lb) have been caught in some European countries.

PIKE

Travelling abroad in search of pike is not particularly common. This is mainly because some of the largest pike are found in Scottish lochs and the trout waters of Ireland, Wales and England.

Sweden is excellent for pike, partly because pike fishing is tightly controlled. In other countries – Germany, for example – pike are eaten.

RUDD

Rudd are found throughout central and southern Europe.

ZANDER

In Europe, from where they originally were imported into England, zander can grow to around 13.6 kg (30 lb) in nutrition-rich waters.

Finding Fish in Running Water – at a Glance

There really is no substitute for getting to know a particular stretch of river. Having said that, this guide will give you an idea of the parts of the river where fish are typically found.

◄ Gravel shallows – dace, roach, grayling

◄ Deep marginal flows and undercut banks – perch

◄ Big depressions – chub, barbel, roach, eel

◄ Lily beds – bream, tench

◄ Weed beds – barbel, eel

◄ Weir pools – barbel

◄ Snags – barbel, eel

◄ Marginal rushes – pike

◄ Creases – many different species of fish, pike in particular

◄ Slow-moving areas – zander

◄ Deep, steady flows – shoals of dace

Finding Fish in Lakes – at a Glance

Obviously, the kinds of lake in which you're likely to be fishing will vary considerably. An overgrown estate lake will be different from day-ticket stillwaters, for instance.

◀ Deep marginal areas – pike, perch, carp, catfish

◀ Beds of lilies – carp, tench

◀ Shallow waters – roach

◀ Edges of rush beds – pike

◀ Bays and inlets, deep water – perch

◀ Around offshore islands – carp

◀ Rush beds – crucian carp

◀ Depressions – eel

◀ Near gravel bars – shoals of bream

◀ Among tree roots – roach

Finding Fish in Gravel Pits – at a Glance

Many fishermen are content to return to the same gravel pit time and time again. This is because of the often wide diversity of fish that can be found in one area of water.

At the same time, really getting to know an area of water is pleasurable and will pay dividends. A gravel pit is an excellent place to learn to understand and predict the behaviour of particular fish.

◀ Weed-free areas – bream, pike

◀ Dense weed – tench

◀ Gravel bars – carp, rudd, bream

◀ Depressions – eel

◀ Deep water – perch

◀ Bankside cover – chub

◀ Gravel bars – roach

◀ Deep holes – rudd

LOOKING AFTER YOUR ROD

It's surprising how many anglers don't bother to clean their rods. It's important to wipe your rods down with a cloth and soapy water as well as regularly replacing any worn rings.

A good way to prevent the joints of your rod sticking is to rub candle wax on the male section. This is the part of the rod that fits inside the hollow end of the next length of rod.

If your rod does get stuck, it's extremely difficult to pull the sections apart by yourself. Ask another angler to help you. Both of you grip the rod on one side of the joint with one hand and the other side of the joint with the other hand.

With both of you pulling steadily, it shouldn't be too difficult to get the rod apart.

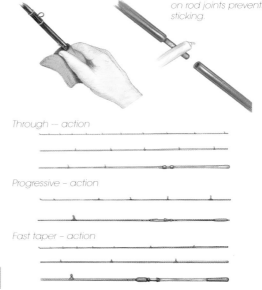

Rubbing candle wax on rod joints prevents sticking.

Through – action

Progressive – action

Fast taper – action

RODS

Rods have three types of action:
Through – for a uniformly smooth curve when playing a fish.
Progressive – rods that give more backbone and increasing power build-up in the butt to control larger fish.
Fast taper – these are very stiff in the butt and have extremely flexible tips, designed for long casting and picking up fine line.

Ideally, you should have a selection of rods for different circumstances. It makes sense to buy one at a time, live with it for a while and expand your collection gradually.

Centrepin

Fixed Spool

Multiplying

You ought to aim to have one of each of the basic types of reel:

Fixed spool – the most common type.

Centrepin – for trotting. Many anglers also use them when ledgering for barbel.

Closedface – for difficult conditions and strong winds.

Multipliers – when you're trotting for pike or fishing for big catfish, for example, and need a large amount of heavy line.

Before buying reels – or any other tackle – ask your dealer for advice.

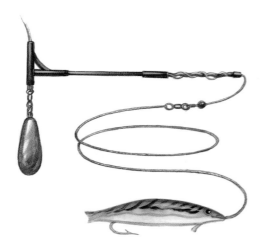

LINES

Modern filament lines are produced to a very high standard, with remarkably narrow diameters and dramatically increased breaking strain. Some of the new fluorocarbon lines are almost invisible in water.

Whatever you're using as your main line, change it regularly. All lines deteriorate over time especially if they're exposed to the sun. Lines ought to be renewed three times a season.

POLES

Poles are used to catch small and medium fish close in on a fixed length of line. They give better float control and bait presentation than rods, as well as improved fish-to-bite ratio. There are two main types of pole:

Long poles – these have detachable sections that mean you can fish at different lengths and with any length of line up to the full length of the pole.

Whips – short, telescopic poles with fine, flexible 'flick tips' for casting and playing fish where the line is attached directly to the tip.

When it comes to choosing your pole or whip, bear in mind that the cheapest poles are made out of glass fibre and the most expensive out of carbon fibre. The more carbon, the lighter and thinner the pole will be.

For long poles, look for lightness, rigidity and balance. With whips, find a pole that's rigid in the bottom sections with a soft tip.

Poles and whips are dealt with in more detail in the pole fishing section on page 108.

FLOATS

Fishing with floats is one of most popular coarse fishing methods. Although there are many types of float fishing it's essential that the float you choose is the right one for the job.

Floats used in rivers will be heavier higher up the stem for stability and riding a current. The weight in stillwater floats is lower down to counter the effects of drift.

For maximum sensitivity, your float also needs to be shotted correctly.

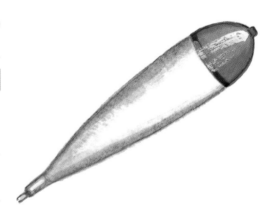

LURES

Lures imitate the behaviour of the prey of predatory fish. Most predators react strongly to violent movement and vibration, the factors behind lure design and use.

In the 'fishing for predators' section (page 114), all kind of lures and their use are described in more detail.

HOOKS

There's a huge choice of hooks on the market. The best thing to do is to experiment with hooks until you find those that suit the kind of fishing you want to do. You can ask your tackle dealer for advice but the following table will give you an idea of which hooks to choose for what purposes.

Standard hook

Wire hook

82

TYPE OF FISHING	HOOKS	COMMENTS
1. BIG CARP	Sizes 2 to 6, beak point, in-curved	Continental boilie
2. PIKE	Sizes 4 to 8, barbed treble hooks	Extra strong
3. OTHER SPECIES	Sizes 4 to 8, beak point, in-curved	Continental boilie, large baits
4. GENERAL FEEDER	Sizes 12 to 16, round bend	Carbon specimen
5. FEEDER, STRONG FISH	Sizes 12 to 16, beak point	Super spades
6. FEEDER, ROACH, DACE	Sizes 14 to 18, beak point	Super spades, ready tied
7. FLOAT FISH, FLAKE	Sizes 8 to 12, crystal bend	Specimen crystal hookbait
8. FLOAT FISH, CASTER	Sizes 16 or 18, crystal bend	Carbon caster hookbait

Bait

Some of the most effective fishing in the summer months is carried out freelining – fishing without weight or floats – using natural baits.

Fishing with natural bait is typically mobile, moving from swim to swim, and it's the recommended way to fish for a number of species.

Natural bait can also be made more effective with a wide range of flavours, colours, enhancers and oils.

LOBWORMS AND REDWORMS

These are extremely effective and simple to find and keep.

On a calm night after steady rain, go out onto close-cropped grass two hours after dark with a torch. Pull the worm gently out of its hole without breaking it – broken worms don't survive.

If you want to make sure of a good supply of redworm, make a compost heap of grass cuttings, leaves, kitchen waste and animal manure.

Keep worms in moist soil with damp moss.

SLUGS

Slugs are perfect for chub. Collect slugs on the morning you're going fishing and keep them fresh in a bait box with some damp green leaves like lettuce, out of the sun.

COCKLES, PRAWNS AND SHRIMP

These are excellent bait but they're fragile and expensive. Only use fresh, shelled cockles.

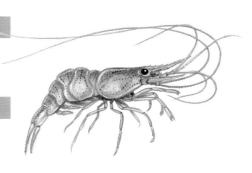

MAGGOTS AND CASTERS

The most popular maggots are the large grubs of the big bluebottle meat fly, pinkies – greenfly larvae, and squatts – housefly larvae.

Bluebottle maggots are the most common hookbait. Pinkies and squatts can be used as hookbait but are more commonly particle attractors in groundbaits or for swimfeeders.

Casters are maggots in the chrysalis stage. They're among the most effective baits for all coarse fish, both in summer and winter, particularly combined with hemp, and you can use them with a swimfeeder.

BREAD

Bread is one of the most versatile baits. If you're using farmhouse crust as bait make sure it's very tough. For hookbait, tear off a piece of crust with a good chunk of bread attached.

Mashed bread is used for looser feeding. Handfuls of fresh, squeezed breadcrumbs will keep a swim primed. Liquidised bread is even more attractive to fish and more economical.

LUNCHEON MEAT

One of the most widely-used baits for many species, particularly chub and barbel, luncheon meat should be used straight from the tin in 2.5 cm (1 in.) cubes.

Luncheon meat becomes bland and unappealing to fish if it's been left on the hook all day and there have been no bites, so remember to change it.

SAUSAGE MEATS

Barbel find these particularly attractive, as do chub, roach and bream. They can either be used on their own or as part of a paste. Prepared sausages such as pepperoni or salami are effective and keep indefinitely.

PASTES

Pastes are extremely versatile, whether you make them yourself or buy them. Making your own paste means you can experiment until you arrive at the right consistency.

Bread paste is cheap, easy to make and effective.

Meat paste is made with sausage meat, finely chopped tinned foods, or soft pet food and mixed with breadcrumbs, biscuit meal or soya flour.

Cheese paste is great for chub, barbel, bream, carp, tench and roach. Make it by mixing cheddar, Danish blue and frozen pastry mix, folding them in together.

Hemp paste is good for taking barbel and chub. An additional advantage is that eels don't like it. To make hemp paste, crush hemp and mix with shortcrust pastry.

Synthetic pastes
Use water or eggs and a mix like Promix for your base. Add liquid or powdered flavours, colours or sweeteners. These can be curry or cheese powder and powdered crawfish or mussel.

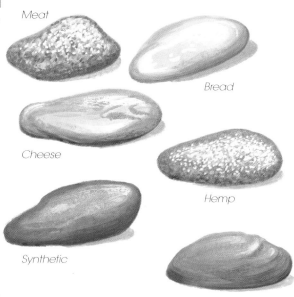

Meat

Bread

Cheese

Hemp

Synthetic

Chocolate

You can also try ingredients like tinned meat or fish with a bulk-binding agent. Believe it or not, wafer chocolate bars mixed with breadcrumbs get good results.

PARTICLE BAITS

Fish like large quantities of food, or particles, like bloodworm colonies. You can get the same effect by saturating a small area with a decent number of particles.

Particle baits should also be big enough to be used on their own or with two or three others on a big hook. Try sweet corn, chickpeas, tiger nuts or even mini boilies.

MASS BAITS

The more bait you use, the better chance you have of attracting fish. Individual pieces of mass bait need to be a lot smaller than particle bait. You can use hempseed, dari, tares, wheat and pearl barley.

Mass baits can also be glued to a large hook.

A word of warning – if you're using commercial mass baits, prepare them according to the instructions. They can be lethal to fish if you don't.

Mass bait glued to a hook

BOILED BAITS

'Boilies' have revolutionised carp fishing. There are plenty of excellent commercial boilies available but specialists prefer to make their own.

You can either add ingredients to a commercially available base or create something from scratch. Use birdseed, mixed groundnuts, fish meals, milk products or a combination.

Before you buy a base mix discuss what you want to achieve with your supplier.

Boilies

FLOATING BAITS

Used to attract surface-feeding fish, floating baits include boilies converted to floaters by baking them, high-protein floaters, floating pet foods, crusts of bread and lobworms.

A boilie, floating bait

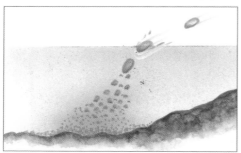

Groundbaiting, creating a feed carpet using bread.

Prebaiting is preparing a swim with bait hours, days and sometimes weeks before fishing. Groundbaiting means introducing bait or creating a feed carpet before, or during, a session.

The most simple type of groundbait is bread but there is a wide range of varieties commercially available.

GROUNDBAITING

Groundbait is used to attract fish, to carry other feed baits into the swim and to hold fish near the hookbait. The type and consistency of groundbait – from cloudy through to heavy and binding – will vary according to conditions.

For instance, cloudy groundbaits are normally used in stillwaters where they also pull fish up off the bottom.

Groundbait is very light so don't struggle to throw it great distances. It's better to learn to use a catapult.

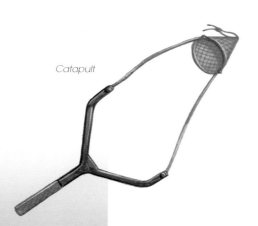

Catapult

Other Useful Equipment

Apart from the fundamentals such as tackle, there's a whole range of equipment to make coarse fishing a comfortable and pleasurable experience.

UMBRELLAS, BIVVIES

You'll often need protection from the elements, especially if you're intending to spend a fair amount of time in one spot. You can buy anything from a standard umbrella to an extremely comfortable bivvie.

If you're river fishing and want to stay mobile, you can do without an umbrella if you've invested in good-quality protective clothing and waterproof gear.

At the most sophisticated end of the market, you can buy double-skinned bivvies with built-in groundsheets that provide a great deal of comfort. You can accessorise bivvies like these with anything from mosquito nets to front tunnels where you can store all kinds of equipment.

FOLDING CHAIRS, BEDCHAIRS AND SEAT BOXES

Always take a fully-sprung, low, comfortable chair when you're planning a long session. The key thing with a low chair is to make sure that it has anti-sink wide feet to stop it sinking it into soft mud.

A bedchair is necessary for overnight sessions. The best kind of bedchairs fold almost completely flat and have three sets of adjustable legs for good stability. Look for a bedchair which has a firm locking position so that you can put the headrest in the position you want.

A seat box is often more convenient than a folding chair because you reduce the amount of gear·you carry. They're often higher which may be more comfortable.

CLOTHING

You need light, comfortable, breathable and 100 per cent waterproof clothing. Whatever you buy, make certain outer garments are at least one size too big so you can wear thermal clothing underneath.

In winter, pay particular attention to keeping your head, hands and feet warm. You should always wear a decent hat. Neoprene gloves, fingerless or otherwise, are good.

For your feet, moonboots or thigh waders are excellent in winter.

92

NETS

Any landing nets or keepnets you purchase should be made of the softest possible material to avoid damaging fish.

When you're fishing for smaller species, especially on rivers, you'll need spoon-shaped landing nets. These are less likely to get tangled in vegetation. With this kind of net, it's always worth using a telescopic handle.

Weigh slings, retention systems, unhooking mats

WEIGH SLINGS

Specialist anglers keep fish they want to photograph in carp sacks. The most useful of these are the lightweight, compact combination sack/weigh slings. You can easily stuff them into small spaces.

Always use an unhooking mat when laying fish on banks, particularly those of gravel pits, are hard and bumpy.

OTHER USEFUL EQUIPMENT

Tackle Box

There are certain things any angler needs for a well-equipped tackle box.

LINE, SHOT, WEIGHTS AND A DISPENSER

Plenty of spare line, non-toxic shot, ranging from small to large and a dispenser, as well as small ledger weights like an Arlesey Bomb.

PLIERS

These allow you to position shot perfectly on line.

HOOKS

Packets of size 10, 16 and 20 barbless hooks.

BEADS

If you're ledgering, you'll need a good quantity of pierced beads.

FLOATS

All-round anglers will have a selection of floats from feature-finder floats through to locslide floats for margin fishing. Build your collection up slowly so you can find out how each behaves and how best to use it. Another thing to bear in mind is that light conditions can vary a great deal.

SWIMFEEDERS

A selection of open-ended swimfeeders.

DISGORGER

These are essential if a fish swallows the hook. Place the disgorger's groove on a taut line and run it into the fish's mouth. It should be easy to nudge gently or turn the hook free.

FORCEPS

Used for removing bigger hooks from specimen fish. If you take up carp or pike fishing, you must have an unhooking mat. You should never lay any fish on hard ground, no matter what size it is.

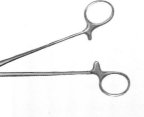

STARLITES

A low-cost way of illuminating a float at night, starlites are activated by breaking a seal and mixing two chemicals to create luminosity. The glow normally lasts for around four hours and is clearly visible within a reasonable range of the bank.

SCALES

If you're fortunate enough to make an exceptional catch, imagine not being able to measure it. Choose between clock-face or spring-balance scales.

SCISSORS AND PENKNIFE

Essential pieces of kit for plenty of different reasons.

CATAPULT

For baiting.

DEPTH PLUMB

To establish where your quarry's feeding.

GUY ROPES AND BIVVY PEGS

If you want to retain your catch to be weighted and photographed, you'll need to have guy ropes and bivvy pegs to help keep it in sufficiently deep water.

95

Float Fishing

Any serious angler will admit that having a float to watch is one of the fundamental pleasures of fishing. Fishing just isn't the same without a float.

There are an enormous number of floats to choose from. This means that the only way you can really get to grips with which floats are best for particular conditions is through a process of trial and error.

Typical types of float include:

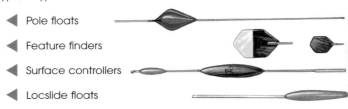

- ◀ Pole floats
- ◀ Feature finders
- ◀ Surface controllers
- ◀ Locslide floats

Regardless of which float you've decided you're most comfortable using, there are certain things to bear in mind.

Your floats shouldn't be too light. It's far better if they're heavier and shotted sensitively.

Whatever you're doing, the key thing is to make sure that the float is clearly visible – light conditions vary constantly. Bright floats are especially important when fishing at night.

TROTTING

Trotting is simply running a float down the current in a number of different situations:

When you're fishing a long, uniform gravelly stretch of river. Under high banks with overhanging foliage or along the junction of two flows that form a crease.

In high water, trotting swims under steep, vertical banks is a good way to fish the species that pack into these undercuts.

For trotting, you should ideally use a 4.2 m (14 ft) rod, Avon or stick floats and a floating line – coated with a silicon spray. Loose feed steadily with maggots or bread.

Make sure that your float just clears the bottom of the shallowest part of the swim. This is laying a float on the streamy water bordering a crease, where you can sometimes catch bigger specimens of fish such as chub or barbel.

STRET PEGGING

You'll use the same tackle as for float fishing with a rod-rest. As you'll be fishing on a tight line you could get savage bites. It is, therefore, important to keep your hand on the rod-butt in case it flips into the river.

Dusk is a good time for stret pegging.

LAYING ON

Laying on is similar to stret pegging but in stillwaters or very sluggish flows. A typical time to use laying on is for tench and bream in overgrown stillwaters at dawn.

Use a waggler float, fished bottom end only with the line sunk between the float and top rod.

THE LIFT METHOD

This is a very precise technique that's excellent for stillwater float fishing. The principle is similar to laying on, but the difference is that the bottom shot is usually fished much closer to the hook.

Lift float fishing at night for crucian carp using an inert waggler fitted with a night-light can be thrilling.

SLIDER FLOAT FISHING

Use a slider when it's impossible to cast a float as far as, and to the depth, you want.

You can convert any float into a slider by making it free-running on the line, stopping it at the right depth with a sliding top knot and bead. This is easily adjusted according to the depth you are fishing at by moving these items.

DRIFT FLOATS

A drift float, used particularly for pike, is designed to catch the wind and be easily visible at long range. Drift float fishing allows you to search water at all ranges and any depths.

Drift float fishing calls for a continually greased line to work well and you need the wind behind you.

CASTING A WAGGLE FLOAT

A waggler is any float attached at the bottom only. Fishing with a waggler is very common on stillwaters when anglers are fishing for roach, tench and carp in particular.

Open-ended swimfeeder

Closed-end swimfeeder

USING A SWIMFEEDER

When you're after bigger fish, especially bream, a swimfeeder filled with groundbait and maggots can be very effective.

WAGGLER FLOATS

Waggler floats come in a series of different shapes and a multitude of sizes. There is a waggler float to suit just about any weather and venue demands you may encounter.

Waggler floats can vary to suit slow-moving water, stillwater, slow-moving water with a long cast and stillwater with a long cast.

Nowadays, the finish on the floats is immaculate and the inclusion of the exact weight the float takes to cock, makes them much easier to use.

Ledgering

Any angler will agree that there are a number of problems with basic freelining.

You have a limited casting range which is dictated by the size of the bait you're using.

Sometimes, detecting a bite is a bit hit and miss because your line is too slack for you to tighten it properly. Your bait can move a little way before you feel it on the rod. This can also result in a fish being deep hooked.

Ledgering is a good way to overcome a lot of these problems. If you've not tried ledgering before, all it involves is using lead on your terminal tackle to increase your casting range.

The lead also tightens up the slack on your line, making it easier to detect early bites.

YOU WILL NEED

◀ A target board to identify bites easily

◀ A rod-rest with multi-position head

◀ A sturdy fixed-spool reel with 1.3–2 kg (3–4 lb) line

◀ Ledger rod-rests

◀ Ledger rod butt with quivertips

◀ A ledger rod of around 3.3 m (11 ft) with interchangeable tips

Ledgering is divided into fixed and running leads.

Try fishing for chub with a simple fixed-lead ledger made by pinching two swan shot onto the line 10 cm (4 in.) from the hook.

To make a basic running lead ledger, use an Arlesey bomb ledger weight with the line free to run through the swivel. This will solve the problem of missing bites at range.

The different permutations of ledgering deal with specific water conditions such as heavy bottom weed. They allow you to adjust bait presentation and give decent bite indications from cautiously biting fish.

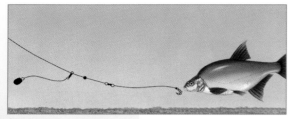
Sliding link leger in action

SLIDING LINK

The weight is mounted on a separate link rather than on the main line. In this way, you can change the amount of lead you're using without breaking down your terminal tackle. You also stand a better chance of recovering the hook in the event of snagging.

Fixed paternoster in action

FIXED PATERNOSTER

Paternosters are weight-forward arrangements with the hook above the lead, designed to overcome problems caused by deep-bottom weed or silt. Use a paternoster for long casting as it is more aerodynamic than a standard link arrangement.

BOLT RIG

The purpose of a bolt rig is, literally, to make the fish bolt with it in their mouth. When educated or nervous fish are biting tentatively, use a bolt rig.

Bolt rig in action

FEEDER BOLT RIG

These are used in stillwaters and the most common is the method feeder rig used very successfully on commercial carp fisheries. A hook is pushed into the side of a ball of mixed feed particles. The idea is that the fish break down the bait and take the hook naturally.

TOUCH LEDGERING

The most sensitive method of detecting bites, these are two methods which take a lot of practice to perfect.

You can either hook a little line over the index finger of the hand holding the rod or take a loop of line in the other hand. It's important to keep the line shallow.

SWIMFEEDER FISHING

Used mainly in stream water to ensure a constant flow of bait down the current, streamer beds are particularly good feeder swims. If you position each cast carefully – between the streamer tresses – loose feed will continually follow the same narrow path. Swimfeeder fishing is ideal for roach, dace, bream, chub and barbel.

UPSTREAM LEDGERING

Nearly all ledgering is done downstream but upstream, using a quivertip, is actually better. When the fish takes the bait downstream all resistance is removed and it holds on for longer. Try looking for hot spots by periodically shifting the lead so that it bumps down the flow. Features like rises in the gravel bed and weed roots will halt its flow.

A misty early morning shot taken by Julian Grattidge, which shows a four rod ledgering set-up for carp.

Combined Float and Ledgering Methods

Float ledgering is a form of laying on where the bottom shot is replaced by a standard ledger weight. The float is shotted so that it rides correctly but is also anchored to the bottom to counter drifting.

This method is ideal for medium- to long-range fishing in very rough conditions and fishing over wide reed margins. It's also very effective when you're fishing for pike or zander with ledgered deadbaits or paternostered livebaits off the bottom.

On some reservoirs like Sywell Reservoir, a famous tench water, ordinary ledgering is actually banned. Here dense weed or lily-bed margins have led to bad practices such as dragging excessively strong lines through the undergrowth and causing damage. As a result of this, only float ledgering is permitted.

DEADBAIT FISHING FOR PIKE

Deadbaits of sea fish are usually used for pike fishing. The most commonly used deadbaits are herrings, sardines, smelts, sprats and mackerel.

Experienced anglers know that when fishing for pike it is vital to bring along a good variety of deadbaits. They know, for instance, that sometimes sardines will fail to produce a bite and it's then necessary to revert to mackerel tail. When mackerel fails to produce a bite, small smelts or sprats could work. Pike prefer different sized baits depending on the time of year and their feeding habits.

Most deadbaits are easier to use when they are partially frozen, because they can be cast further. Therefore, a good cool box is a must for serious anglers.

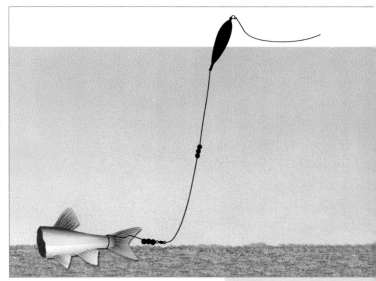

COMBINED FLOAT AND LEDGERING METHODS

Pole Fishing

Pole fishing is increasingly popular among all kinds of anglers.

At its most basic, a pole is simply a rod without a reel and the line attached directly to the end of the pole. There are three types of pole:

Put in – slimmer, softer; the smallest sections fit inside the largest, usually used when fishing to hand, where the length of line you're using is the same as the pole.

Put over – thicker, stiffer; the biggest section fits inside the smallest, these are more commonly used.

Telescopic or whip – used with line a little shorter than the pole attached directly to the tip.

They're used to place bait exactly where you want, particularly in rough conditions.

Spare sections are added to the butt section – unless you're using a telescopic whip – to present bait delicately at different distances. They also give extra cushioning if you hook a bigger fish.

TACKLE

If you're thinking about taking up pole fishing you'll need several items of specialist tackle:

▶ A carbon fibre whip around 3.9 m (13 ft) long

▶ A carbon fibre put in or put over the pole – opinions differ as to which is best, so talk to your tackle dealer

▶ A pole rest

▶ A roller to take the strain of a long pole

▶ Medium pole elastic – your line is attached to elastic running through the top two sections which takes the strain of a catch

▶ Pole floats – smaller and more sensitive than ordinary floats, weight up for running water and down for still

▶ Pole float winders

▶ Rubber pole float winder anchors

▶ Length of silicone pole float rubber

▶ Non-toxic weights and size 10 shot

Using a long pole, especially when fishing to hand with the same length line as the pole, is a bit intimidating at first. It's best to work up to it in stages.

CHOOSING A POLE

When you're choosing a pole, the general principle to remember is that the lighter and stiffer it is the more relaxing it will be to use. You should also consider the type of fishing you'll be doing.

A match angler might pick a stiff, light pole that can be held effortlessly for long periods of time. For carp, a pole with more flexibility in the tip is better. Always buy a carbon fibre pole.

USING A WHIP

The whip really comes into its own when you're match fishing and want to catch a lot of small fish close in. You're not likely to catch large fish with a whip and it's not a good idea to try. If your line breaks you'll leave a hook in the mouth of the fish.

The whip is also typically used on the near side of a canal or the edge of a river.

The important thing to remember with a whip is that you're not able to remove sections when you're fishing.

POLE FISHING

Poles are especially effective in small to medium rivers with wide rush margins. Fish of many species feed tight against this marginal vegetation and you can present bait with a degree of accuracy that's far better than with a rod.

The most successful way to fish with a pole on a river is to follow standard trotting principles. This means keeping a steady trickle of feed going in on the right line, ensuring the right amount and consistency of groundbait.

You also need to make certain that the float follows the current without jerking or being pulled off the line in which the feed is going.

POLE FISHING IN STILL WATERS

On stillwaters, a pole would typically be used if you're after roach and bream. You should, ideally, have a short, light pole or whip for shallower water and a stiffer pole for deeper waters.

When you're using a long pole it's important to make sure you're comfortable. If you're sitting on your box, check that it's at the right height and the roller is positioned correctly.

It's important to use as much line as possible between your pole and float. Fish will be able to see it in shallower water. The less line you have, the fewer sections of pole you'll have to take apart.

SAFETY

Wherever you're using a pole, don't fish under power lines, for obvious reasons, and please take the time to warn others of the risks.

Don't ever use a carbon fibre pole – or rod for that matter – in stormy conditions. There's a very real danger of being struck by lightning.

Fishing for Predators

Going after predatory fish, cunning hunters themselves, is especially challenging and exciting for any angler.

You can use a variety of techniques and baits depending on the fish you're looking for.

LIVEBAITS

Some predatory fish such as pike or zander will be attracted by live coarse fish of the kind they naturally eat. Livebaits should be lightly paternostered and used near a suitable predator fish ambush point – old lily roots, for example.

You can use a roving rig when livebaiting but you need to make sure that your poly ball is big enough. If not, the bait will pull the float under and keep it there. If the float disappears out of sight you won't know if you've got a bite.

DEADBAITS

Deadbaiting is becoming particularly popular as more and more anglers decide that livebaiting is unacceptable.

They're mainly used for pike fishing and the most common are herrings, smelts, sprats and mackerel. Whole sardines are especially good for large fish but need to be frozen. This is why a good cool box is an essential purchase if you're serious about going after predatory fish.

The best freshwater deadbaits are roach, small chub, an eel or lamprey section, small trout or immature pike. Whenever you're freezing deadbait, cut them into sections first.

It's become very popular to flavour deadbait with fish oils such as mackerel, smelt or eel. Flavouring deadbait can make a real difference when you're fishing on large areas of windswept stillwater where currents below the surface will waft the trails around.

Deadbaits can also be coloured to make them more attractive to predatory fish.

LURES

Any predatory fish can be caught using a lure and you can even occasionally take fish that aren't normally predatory – carp, bream and barbel, for instance.

Lures imitate the prey of predatory fish, not necessarily in appearance but more in behaviour. Most predators react strongly to sudden movement and vibration and it's these factors that are mimicked by lures.

One of the good things about lure fishing is the fact that you don't need much additional equipment. If you do become keen on the technique, a bait-casting rod of around 2.7 m (9 ft) is ideal. You also need a good, strong reel that is ideally vibration free and has a reliable fighting drag system.

Thin, supple trace wire no less than 6.8 kg (15 lb) is vital but this should be more if you're fishing for pike.

Fishing with lures is most productive, especially in the warmer months and is extremely exciting. Going after pike using a surface lure is a particular challenge.

More experienced anglers like the challenge of using sub-surface lures, where timing the strike is all about feel.

FISHING FOR PREDATORS

PLUGS

Plugs are wooden, plastic or metal lures that 'swim' or wobble upright through the water imitating the movements of predatory fish prey. They're particularly used for pike when they usually mimic sick or injured fish. Some look like mice or frogs.

Shallow-diving floater

The key thing is that the plug provokes an instinctive strike. There are four basic types of plug:

Shallow-diving floaters – designed to dive a few centimetres.

Deep-diving floats – dive very steeply when you retrieve them.

Deep-diving floater

Adjustable depth floaters – where the diving depth varies each time you retrieve.

Sinkers – sink when you first cast them in and rise higher in the water the quicker they're retrieved.

Suspending plugs are also good when fishing for zander.

Adjustable depth floater

If you're serious about fishing with plugs, it's important to buy a complete range rather than picking them up at random, although many people collect plugs almost for their own sake.

Plugs tend to work best in summer and autumn when pike and their prey are both active.

117

SPINNERS AND SPOONS

Spinners are a type of lure with a rotating blade to create vibration. Of the three types available, the buzzer is extremely successful in attracting pike to strike. They're a must for your lure collection.

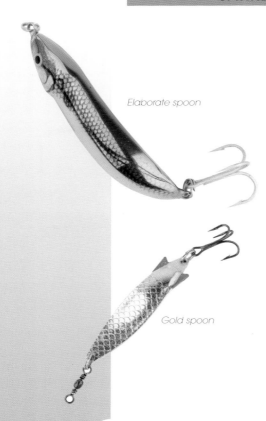

Elaborate spoon

Gold spoon

Spoons are simply flat pieces of metal shaped like spoons which wobble when they're retrieved.

The key to using spinners and spoons effectively is how quickly and how much you vary your retrieve after you've cast. Your retrieve should be calm, slow and controlled and you should occasionally flip the lure to one side to create additional vibration.

You would normally choose a lightweight spinner with a revolving aluminium blade.

SPINNING FOR PIKE

Look first for all the areas where pike are most likely to be – close to cover or ambush points, reedy margins, lily beds and drop-offs at the edges of gravel bars.

The same applies for rivers. Always work upstream and start with your smallest spinner.

118

SPINNING FOR PERCH

Spinning is one of the most effective ways of taking perch in large stillwaters. Perch rely more on visual stimulus than pike so tasselled spinners are particularly effective.

A red tassel imitates the tail of a roach or rudd. In coloured waters, where rudd feed avidly, use a more flashy lure.

When retrieving the spinner try to do so as slowly as possible with occasional bursts of activity. It also helps to bait your hook with lobworm.

Tasselled spinner

SPINNING FOR OTHER SPECIES

A fly spinner – a tiny spinner with the hook dressed as an artificial fly – is effective for taking chub. You can also use fly spoons, which are fly-shaped spoons with a dressed hook attached.

Whichever species you're fishing for, it's important to remember that the shape and thickness of the spinner blade needs to vary according to water conditions. A broad blade is ideal for stillwaters and slow streams. Thinner blades have less resistance and can be used in fast water without the skating on the water surface.

Green and gold spoon

Responsible Fishing

If you take angling seriously there's a code of practice that all responsible anglers follow.

HANDLING FISH

When it comes to careful fish handling, there are a number of basic dos and don'ts:

▶ Always handle fish with wet hands – dry hands will damage the protective coating of a fish

▶ Return fish to the water immediately if possible

▶ Use barbless hooks

▶ Always use a disgorger to remove hooks

▶ Always use a landing net rather than lifting fish out using your line

▶ Fish over 4.5 kg (10 lb) should be weighed using a weigh bag

▶ When you're choosing your swim take extra care if you're in a place where people usually feed waterfowl – their expectations could lead to greater risk of entanglement.

▶ Never leave your rods unattended – it's actually illegal to do so – or with hooks still baited.

▶ Use a hook length of lower breaking strain than the reel line wherever possible.

▶ If you're using a bolt rig or fixed lead, make sure that if the line breaks it won't result in a fish or bird dragging a ledger around.

▶ Use barbless or reduced hooks wherever possible.

▶ Lead weights are illegal in most sizes – apart from No 8 shot or less or more than 28 g (1 oz) – and non-toxic weights are widely available.

▶ When you're fishing, beware of birds swimming into your line or picking up surface baits.

▶ Take great care when you're fishing surface baits like bread or floaters as they may attract waterfowl.

123

REMOVING A HOOK

Sooner or later, most anglers will get a hook stuck in their flesh.

The least painful way of removing a hook is to press down on the shank to reduce the grip of the barb. When you're pressing hardest, jerk the hook straight forward in line with the shank quickly and powerfully.

Using this technique, the barb should slide cleanly out with very little, if any, flesh tearing.

SAFETY

The most common cause of accidents to anglers is wading. When you're wading downstream, always make sure of the depth of the water between you and the bank.

Be very careful around overhead power lines and warn other anglers of the danger.

Essential Products team member Chris Knapper with a perfect Top Pool 23 lb mirror carp.

Current British Coarse Fishing Records

Many anglers, particularly specimen anglers, enjoy keeping up with current British coarse fishing records and matching their catches against them.

126

The records listed here come from The British Coarse Fishing Society and are for the first half of 2003.

TYPE OF FISH	CURRENT BRITISH RECORD
Barbel	8.79 kg (19 lb 6 oz 8 drm)
Bream	8.20 kg (18 lb 5 oz)
Carp	27.67 kg (61 lb)
Chub	3.91 kg (8 lb 10 oz)
Crucian carp	1.87 kg (4 lb 2 oz 8 drm)
Dace	0.56 kg (1 lb 4 oz 4 drm)
Eel	5.04 kg (11 lb 2 oz)
Grayling	1.87 kg (4 lb 2 oz)
Perch	2.51 kg (5 lb 9 oz 8 drm)
Pike	21.23 kg (46 lb 13 oz)
Roach	1.80 kg (4 lb 3 oz)
Rudd	2.09 kg (4 lb 10 oz)
Tench	6.89 kg (15 lb 3 oz)
Zander	8.74 kg (19 lb 5 oz)

CURRENT BRITISH COARSE FISHING RECORDS

Steve Randles displays a superb 1lb 15 oz

Picture credits

Title page: David Miller. 5: Top That!
7-8: Stockbyte. 9: Corel.
11: www.anglersnet.co.uk.
13: David Miller.
14-16: www.anglersnet.co.uk.
18: Stockbyte. 21: David Miller.
24: Map Resources.
25: www.anglersnet.co.uk.
26: Mike Atkinson
27: www.anglersnet.co.uk.
28: Map Resources. 29: Mike Atkinson.
30: www.anglersnet.co.uk.
31: David Miller. 32: Map Resources.
33: Mike Atkinson.
34: www.anglersnet.co.uk.
35: Map Resources. 36: Mike Atkinson.
37: David Miller.
38: (t) Map Resources.,
(b) www.anglersnet.co.uk.
39: Mike Atkinson. 40: Map Resources.
41: Corel. 42: Mike Atkinson.
43: Map Resources. 44: Mike Atkinson.
45: David Miller.
46: (t) Map Resources.,
(b) www.anglersnet.co.uk.
48: David Miller. 49: Map Resources.
50: Mike Atkinson. 51: David Miller.
52: www.anglersnet.co.uk.
53: Map Resources. 54: Mike Atkinson.
55: David Miller. 56: Map Resources.
57: Mike Atkinson. 58: Map Resources.
59: Mike Atkinson. 60: Map Resources.
61: www.anglersnet.co.uk.
62: Mike Atkinson.
63-64: Map Resources. 65: Stockbyte.
66-68: Map Resources. 69: Stockbyte.
71-73: www.anglersnet.co.uk.
75: Corel. 77-78: Mike Atkinson.
79: www.anglersnet.co.uk.
80-96: Mike Atkinson. 97: David Miller.
98-100: Mike Atkinson.
101: Top That! 103-104: Mike Atkinson.
105: www.anglersnet.co.uk.
107: Mike Atkinson.
111-113: www.anglersnet.co.uk.
114: David Miller. 115-119: Top That!.
121: www.anglersnet.co.uk.
122-124: Mike Atkinson. 125: Corel.
126-128: www.anglersnet.co.uk.

Tight Lines!

Hopefully, this book has told you things you didn't know about your favourite pastime. Maybe you're itching to update your tackle and go after fish you've been thinking about for ages. Perhaps you've been reminded that there are techniques you've yet to try or haven't used in far too long.

At the very least, we hope you've been inspired to look at coarse angling from a fresh perspective.

In the words of coarse anglers everywhere: when you next go fishing – tight lines!